End of the World

Book of Daniel Prophecy

By

David Zephaniah

Contents

- Prince Daniel 5
- Young men's courage 7
  - The test of wisdom 11
- King's riddle 13
- Daniel solves king's riddle 20
- The cruelty of the pagan world 27
- The furnace miracle 32
- The King goes mad 35
- The evil empire 39
- The nation of Israel 49
- The fall of Babylonian 55
- The Lion's den miracle 60
- Jerusalem's destruction 66
- End of the World prophecy 72
- The fate of the world nations 91
- Inspirational Material 96

Inspirational Material

I want to emphasize that this book is based upon the Book of Creation. The Book of Creation is the only book in existence that was authored by the Maker Himself. All other Bibles were written by men at much later time. Those people used some parts of the Book of Creation to legitimize their books, but that is all.

I came to believe that every word in the Book of Creation is true. The stories in the Book of Creation are not figurative. They are literal and factual. Our Creator in not some powerless pagan deity; He is all powerful Creator, who stretched this universe and created the spirit of men by His words alone. When He says something, it is done. There is absolutely nothing He cannot do.

One might contemplate the ultimate question; if the Creator is all powerful, why is our world is full of hardship, violence, injustice, pain, etc.?

The answer is actually very simple. World creation

has a purpose. Its purpose will be realized at the end of the current world. Humans are bestowed with free will. We have Good Inclination (Godly), and Bad Inclination (animalistic). This world that we live in is merely a test that God administers to test our souls. The purpose of our current life drama is to overcome the bad inclination and better ourselves. That can be accomplished only by observing the Book of Creation Commandments (Mitzvas in Hebrew).

The world today is in a bad shape because most of the people in the world are overcome by their animalistic souls and practice immorality, crime, immodesty, dishonesty, etc. They have created this terrible world, because they do not follow the Book of Creation commandments, or at least 7 Noahide laws.

During this lifetime we are judged according to every word, thought and action. This process goes on until we die. Some of us are destined to come back to this earth again to correct our errors. Some of us who are overwhelmingly good or bad are already sentenced after our deaths. Regardless of who we are, our souls exist in a different realm until the end. The final judgment of each individual will be handed down at the appointed time, when this world ends.

At the world's end, some souls will be erased from existence, because they merited bad sentence. Some extra bad souls will be brought back to life for the eternal suffering in the "pit".

The righteous people will also be brought back (resurrected) for the eternal life on this earth. They will be mostly Jews, who observe the Book of Creation and the righteous among the gentile nations.

In this lifetime, people who follow the teachings of the Book of Creation are blessed with great lives and great wisdom. They do not turn to scientists when it comes to family relationships, happiness, child care, friendship, and other profound subjects. They rely on the teachings of the Book of Creation 100%. As a result they have great family relationships, love, happiness and satisfaction.

People that observe the Book of Creation Commandments, are free of crime and violence, because they get the protection of the Maker in their lifetime! For example, if the righteous person is present when and where the terrorist is trying to detonate a bomb, the bomb will not detonate. When a righteous person is driving towards a fiery car crash, he/she will avoid it by few seconds. Since the Maker controls absolutely everything, the events are happening seamlessly. Nobody can notice miracles that are happening every day. The Maker is all powerful and ultimately just. Everything happens for a reason. We are unable to understand many things, but this is because it is not our business to know.

I want the reader to know, God is the only true fortune teller. He is the only one that knows the future.

Below are some great websites for people who would like to learn more. You don't have to be Jewish to rip great benefits. However, if you want to go all the way and make a real effort, there are even greater rewards beyond this harsh lifetime.

Prince Daniel

The story begins in the year 600BC, at the height of the Babylonian Empire, with the leadership of king Nebuchadnezzar. The humongous Babylonian army invaded and conquered the tiny Jewish kingdom of Judah. King Jehoiakim of Judah was left in power; however, the Babylonians imposed a heavy tax upon them

 Babylonians also exiled thousands of Jewish captives, including the king's family, nobility, and the leaders of the army. They left only the poorest of the people in the land.

King Nebuchadnezzar gave an order to his chief military officer Ashpenaz to bring along many good looking children of Israel of royal and noble descent. He wanted healthy children with no blemishes and of handsome appearance that had the wisdom and knowledge, were able to express their thoughts, and who had mental capacity to understand, and had good manners.

The king wanted them to be trained for service in his palace. It was customary for the Babylonians to take young children, boys and girls, from the countries they conquered, and to teach them to serve the king in the palace. Some of these children were destined to occupy a prominent place in the Babylonian court.

Once in the king's palace, those children were fed daily with the king's food and wine, taught the language and customs of Babylonian priests and trained in the arts of service to the king. They were to be taught for three years. After the training, they were to be prepared to stand in front of the King and serve him.

Among those young children there was a 15-year-old handsome prince named Daniel. The Babylonians also took three of Daniel's best friends of about the same age. Their names were: Hananiah, Mishael and Azariah. The chief officer gave them all Babylonian names. He called Daniel Belteshazzar, Hananiah-Shadrach, Mishael-Meshach, and Azariah-Abed-Nego. All four of those children were descendants of royal Jewish families. They were quite young when they got torn away from their homes and brought to Nebuchadnezzar's royal palace. One can imagine the pain and tears of mothers, whose children got lost to a hostile, far-away land. The memory of tormented faces of his mother and father would haunt Daniel for years.

Young men's courage

Daniel's trip to Babylon was full of challenges and suffering. He and his three friends were part of a group of about 100 young captives from the country of Judah. The children were crammed together in small wagons, traveling through the hot desert. They survived drinking water, eating bread and vegetables because they refused to eat non-kosher meat. Since they had each other, they felt stronger and tried to maintain a positive attitude, helping each other and other kids. The four young men believed that better days were ahead, and a brighter future was awaiting them. They were hoping that one day in the near future, they would be allowed to go back home, to live with their families again. Daniel always tried to cheer them up, telling those stories of their ancestors, which he heard at the holiday gatherings in his home.

The journey from Jerusalem to the Land of Shinar took about 6 months. Daniel and his three friends were brought to the king's palace, along with the other younglings, in order to be trained in the customs of the Babylonian priests, and to serve the king of Babylon.

Since Daniel and his three friends were devoted Jews, they refused to eat the king's food or drink his wine. They were observing strictly kosher rules and insisted to keep it so, even if their life depended on it. Daniel risked his life by refusing to break kosher diet. He gave a request to be allowed to eat vegetarian food only. The Chief Officer was kind enough to answer because he felt compelled to do so. He said to Daniel: "I would like to help you, but I fear that if my king finds out that you and your friends don't eat his food, and you are not well, he will order to kill us all".

The Book of Creation indicates that faith in Creator means that you will have such a strong conviction, that you will risk your life, in order to uphold the commandments. That is how you get the attention of Creator.

Daniel, together with his friends; Hananiah, Mishael and Azariah replied with confidence that they would be fine to eat only vegetables and suggested that the chief officer tested them for 10 days. Daniel sent a letter to the chief officer. The letter read: "Test us for ten days. We will not eat the king's food for ten days. We will eat only beans and vegetables. You can review our health and looks. You will see that our Creator will protect us and keep us in a good shape. At the end of ten days, compare us with other youths that ate the king's food".

The chief officer, in his kindness, agreed to give it a shot and ordered to feed them vegetarian meals. It was highly unusual for him to do so. He was not a pleasant person. The Bible says that he agreed because of the divine intervention.

At the end of the ten days, the four friends looked more attractive and healthy than the other youths, who ate the king's meat. Once the king's steward and the chief officer saw that, they allowed the four friends to eat the food they wanted as it was the custom of the Jews.

Daniel and his friends were unique to Creator because they had conviction and faith. Regardless to the terrible events that they witnessed, with the destruction of their kingdom, oppression of their people, and separation from their loved ones, they kept their faith in Creator. The four children did not have a doubt in their mind that all the terrible events that were happening around them had a reason and purpose. They thought that it was punishment for inequities of many Jewish people, by their Creator. Daniel, Hananiah, Mishael and Azariah knew that their Creator would not abandon them, and at the right time they would be free people again.

The truly faithful person never blames Creator for their misfortunes. They assume that Creator is always right, with no exceptions.

Because of their firm belief and faith, Creator gave the four of them unique skills and knowledge and understanding in the wisdom and writing, in different languages. When they went to sleep, an angel visited them in a dream and gave them information, in order to increase their knowledge about the local customs and languages. In addition, Creator gave Daniel an ability to decipher visions and dreams. All four of them became outstanding and smart boys.

Daniel learned that through the dreams, Creator is giving us wisdom when we deserve it.

The life in the castle was not so terrible for the four boys. The Babylonian empire believed in tapping into the best young talent. For the Babylonians, the youth from the kingdom of Judah, was an integral part of the wealth that they robbed from the kingdom of Judah, after their conquest.

The test of wisdom

Three years passed. Time came for Daniel, Hananiah, Mishael and Azariah to appear before the king. They were to be tested in their skill and knowledge, in order to determine, what role in the palace would be suitable for each one of them.

It was a festive and entertaining event. It was a large gathering at the king's main courtyard, with the presence of many local dignitaries, governors, viziers and officers. The children of the king were present, as well as the queen, and king's many beautiful concubines. Everyone wore colorful and stylish garments. There were hundreds of dignitaries and guests, from all over the kingdom. The guests were served fancy cuisines from different corners of the kingdom. King Nebuchadnezzar was in a good spirit.

The whole affair was extremely colorful and beautiful. There were about a hundred good-looking boys and girls, who appeared in front of the king that day. They all completed their grooming process that went on for three years, and they were all familiar with the customs and the language of Chaldeans. Daniel was the most handsome among them. All the women of the palace were trying to get his attention.

In order to evaluate the youths in their knowledge and skills, King brought many of his wise men, to see who was smarter and more knowledgeable. Amongst the wise men were Astrologers, Demonologists, Necromancers and Soothsayers.

In every test and competition that the wise men administered, to the youths in front of them, in wisdom, understanding and the secret arts, the king found that Daniel and his 3 friends were 10 times smarter, and more knowledgeable than any other child that were present. Those four children shone like stars, and immediately attracted the attention of the king. They were smarter and more knowledgeable than all the Necromancers and Astrologers in his whole kingdom.

 When king witnessed their ability, he ordered to assign them to the high positions in the palace, in charge of the other servants of the king and the position of the spiritual advisers.

Daniel did not know at the time that he would stay in Babylonian castle for many years to come. He tried to live a normal life. However, his mind was longing for his home country and his family. He prayed every day, and asked Creator to forgive the Jews for their transgressions.

King's riddle

For six years, King Jehoiakim of Judah pretended to serve the king of the Babylon, however, in his mind, he was planning a rebellion. He totally ignored the warnings of the prophet Jeremiah, who foretold the invasion of the Babylonians, and claimed that this was Creator's punishment. Jeremiah said that Creator has issued this sentence because many Jews reverted to the idol worship.

Jeremiah said that it was useless to oppose the Babylonians because Creator had already decided to let them dominate the kingdom of Judah.

Despite of Jeremiah's warnings, King Jehoiakim made an alliance with king Necho of Egypt, who also had revenge against Babylonians in his mind, and together they tried to rebel. They failed miserably. As the result of this rebellion, Babylonians destroyed a part of Jerusalem and the God's Temple. Everything happened exactly as Jeremiah predicted. King Jehoiakim fell captive and was taken to the land of

Shinar, home of the Babylonian idol gods. Along with the king, the Babylonians took some of the sacred ritual vessels of silver and gold from the Temple in Jerusalem. Jehoiakim died on the way to Shinar, from a cause that is not exactly known.

Daniel received this prophecy 2 years after the Temple destruction in Jerusalem. It was Daniel's 8th years in captivity in Babylon. The rumors of the Temples destruction arrived to the Jewish captives in Babylon. They were totally devastated and demoralized, Daniel among them. Because of his unique wisdom, Daniel already got promoted to the Wise Man job and enjoyed a comfortable life. Nevertheless he longed for his family, and the beautiful country of Judah.

After hearing about the Temple's destruction, Daniel was depressed and distraught for weeks. He was wandering, along with his three friends, Hananiah, Mishael, and Azariah, for what reason Creator imposed such a harsh punishment upon the Jewish people. He made sure that he prayed every morning and evening.

Shortly after the Temples destruction, King Nebuchadnezzar of Babylon started having an unusually frightening and reoccurring dream. As a result, he was extremely depressed. His sleep got interrupted many times because of the scary dream. The worst thing about this dream was that once he woke up, he could not remember it. However, he felt terrified each time.

This reoccurring dream went on for months and finally one morning, the king decided to go ahead and gather his best wise people, Necromancers, Astrologers, magicians, Sorcerers and the Chaldean priests so they could tell him what the dream was and to clarify its meaning. That beautiful summer morning, the wise men came and assembled before the king.

The king, who looked visibly distressed, restless and tired, addressed the wise men: "I've been dreaming a terrible dream over and over again, and I am extremely disturbed. I need to find out what it means because I feel anxious and edgy". He was convinced that his best wise men would be able to help him figure out what was going on, and what his dream meant.

Chaldeans, who were the head of the wise people, and were ready to serve the king, spoke and greeted the king in Aramaic: "May the king live forever! We are your servants. Tell us your vision and we shall tell you the meaning and the meanings".

The king has replied in frustration: "I do not remember the dream. All I remember is that it was terrifying. I expect you, my wise men, to tell me what the dream was about, because, then and there, I will know for sure that you know the interpretation and meaning, as well. If you do not tell me the dream and its meaning, I will have you killed, I will order to cut your body to pieces, and I will turn your houses into the dung heap, as a sign of dishonor." And the evil king went on saying, with extremely serious and grim expression: "However if you tell me the dream and its interpretation, you will receive lavish gifts, and tremendous honor from me because this matter of this dream is extremely crucial to me".

The Chaldean priests looked terrified. They were well

aware of king Nebuchadnezzar's cruelty, and they consulted each other for a few moments. At that time, their leader, a middle-aged man dressed in purple robes replied the second time as if he did not understand what it is that the king was asking of them: "O' king, please tell us the dream that you had, and we shall be glad to interpret its meaning to you."

At this time, the king was very angry. After taking a deep breath, he replied back with a sarcastic tone: "I have a feeling that all of you will get killed because I already told you that I do not remember the dream, and you are continually asking me to tell it to you. I am warning you that if you do not tell me the dream and its meaning, there is but one sentence for you, which is death. I will give you time until the night to give me an answer. I know that if you tell me what the dream was, you will surely know the meanings as well because it will mean that you are not fake and corrupted wise men."

The Chaldeans were terribly frightened and replied: "The response was appropriate, O' king, in view of the fact that there was never a king in the history of the world, who asked anything like you ask of the wise men. Your question is impossible to answer, there are no men in existence who can answer it .Only angels would know, and we have no way of getting in touch with them."

Although the sorcery and magic is real, they have a limited power. For example, they could interpret a dream for you, but they could not tell you what dream you have dreamt.

The king was furious. In his momentary rage and anger, he ordered to kill all the wise men of Babylon, starting that night. This execution order included Daniel and his friends because they were wise men as well. The order went out to the chief Executioner of the king, and he instructed his people to look for all the wise men in the kingdom of Babylon, in order to kill them as urgently as possible. The word got out in the kingdom that wise men were about to be slain, and the public became gripped with panic and fear. The wise men were revered and depended upon by the royalty as well as the general population. The kingdom was in disarray.

Once Daniel heard about the king's decree, he contacted Arioch, the King's Chief Executioner, who was in charge on the quest to kill all the wise men of Babylon. Once in front of him, he said to Arioch: "What is the reason for this cruel and wild decree to be issued so hastily?"

Arioch, who looked distraught himself, explained Daniel that the king was extremely angry, because he felt deceived by the wise men. He wanted someone to tell him his dream and its meaning. He said that those dreams overtook the king and obsessed him.

After hearing Arioch's response, Daniel felt that he had to do something in urgency. He wanted to save himself, his friends and the wise men of Babylon from certain death. He immediately requested to have the audience of the king, and told Arioch that he would be able to tell the dream and its meaning to the king.

While awaiting Arioch's response, Daniel prayed to Creator, asking him to reveal the king's dream and its meaning. He prayed, so his friends and he would not perish, along with all the wise men of Babylon.

The secret of the dream was revealed to Daniel, shortly thereafter in a dream. Daniel fell asleep for a few minutes. In a dream, he saw the king's dream. Creator also showed him that the kingdom of Babylon had an allotted time to exist.

Upon awakening, Daniel understood that Creator decides which king [or president] rules each kingdom, and how long each kingdom exists. He went ahead and blessed Creator for the wisdom He gave him. He spoke up and prayed out loud:

"May the name of Creator be blessed; for everlasting. He is the one that changes times and seasons on earth. He removes kings and sets up kings as he wishes. He grants wisdom to the wise, and knowledge to the one who understands. He reveals deep and mysterious things that are unknown to men. He always knows what lurks in the dark, and the light itself dwells within him. To you, O Creator of my forefathers, Abraham, Isaac and Jacob, I give thanks and praise, for you have given me wisdom and strength, and now you have let me know what I have requested of you, for the matter of the king you have let me know..."

Daniel solves king's riddle

Daniel was quite relieved. He was happy and excited from the fact that by solving the king's dream, he was able to save many lives. He entered the Chief Executioner's chamber and told the guards that he was on the mission of extreme urgency. Once brought in, he looked Arioch right in the eye and said, "Do not harm the wise men of Babylon. Bring me before the king right now and I shall interpret the dream for him."

Arioch was an exceptionally brutal man. He was a 6'5 killing machine, with a mean face. He was extremely pleased to hear the news because he felt distraught by the fact that he had to slay the wise men of Babylon. Indeed, it was a truly bizarre job for him, but nevertheless, regardless to his personal feelings and opinion, he could not disobey the authority of his king. So, he brought Daniel before the king immediately and addressed the king, "My lord, I found a man of the exiles of Judah who claims he can explain the dream and its meaning. He seems remarkably confident."

The king was seating on his throne with red-shot eyes, wondering if he made the right decision, by ordering to kill all the wise men of Babylon. He was extremely excited to hear that someone was able to explain his riddle. Daniel was his favorite wise man, and he knew him well. He asked Daniel if he would be able to solve the complex riddle, something that no other wise men in Babylon could do.

 Daniel answered, "The answer you're seeking is not known to any Necromancer, Astrologer, Demonologist or any other wise man in the world. However, there is an almighty God in heavens, who reveals secrets to me, and through me, He wants to let you, king Nebuchadnezzar, know that your dream refers to the future events. Creator knows what is on your mind and what you are constantly thinking about. You are worried, and want to know who will rise and rule the kingdom of Babylon after your death."

Creator knows your thoughts. Imagine yourself how powerful Daniel was in the eyes of the king; by guessing his thoughts, dream, and the interpretation.

Daniel paused for a moment. Since the king was

silent, listening intensively to every word that Daniel had to say, Daniel went on describing the dream to the king.

"O king, in your dream, you were in a strange and unfamiliar place, without the security of your personal guards around you, and without a sword in your hand. As you were frightfully looking around and exploring, you saw a giant statue of a royal man standing opposite of you. The statue was about 30 feet tall and stood on a large base. Its form had an outstanding splendor and it was truly disturbing. You felt hypnotized by its presence, and started looking at it closely. You wanted to know whom the statue represented and why it was there. You noticed that the head of the statue was made of fine gold. Its chest and arms were made of silver, and its belly and thighs were made of copper. Its legs were made of iron and its feet were made of iron and clay. "

"While you were still looking terrified at the image opposite of you, a large stone was cut from the ground next to you, by an unseen hand. The unseen hands lifted the stone from the ground, and threw it at the statue, striking it to its feet. The impact immediately crumbled the feet, and the whole statue came down with the loud noise, crashing to the ground, breaking into hundreds of pieces. Moments later, all of those crumbled pieces were blown away like leaves in the wind. Nothing was left of the statue. The stone which struck the image remained in place and after a few minutes, it grew into an enormous mountain which filled the whole visible world. This is the dream that you dreamed"

At the end of days, all the countries that are in existence right now will be gone as if they never existed.

The king's face lit up because he had an immediate sense of relief and satisfaction. He knew that Daniel was telling the truth, and was extremely excited because he could not wait to hear the interpretation. Daniel paused for a few seconds and then followed with the dream interpretation.

"O king, the mighty Creator gave you a powerful and prominent kingdom. The statue in the dream is a metaphor and symbolizes the future events. The golden head of the statue symbolizes you because your kingdom is vast and extremely prominent in the world.

After your death, your two sons will rule the kingdom of Babylon for a while more. When your youngest son, Belshazzar, dies, a new kingdom will raise, which will take the ruling power from your descendants. However, the new kingdom will be smaller and humbler than your kingdom, as silver is lower and humbler than gold, and you saw that the chest of the statue, which is after the head, was of silver. So will be a kingdom of Media and Persia, which will replace the kingdom of Babylon, be humbler than the kingdom of king Nebuchadnezzar.

After those kingdoms, another will rise, as tough as the copper torso of the statue and it will be the kingdom of Alexander Macedon the Greek, and it will be extremely powerful. It will rule over the entire earth.

After that empire comes to an end, four kingdoms will emerge from that kingdom. These kingdoms will be as strong as the iron thighs of the statue. These kingdoms will be divided kingdoms. When the time comes, they will disintegrate as well, and as they crumble, they will shatter and crumble all the nations within it and scatter them all around the world.

In the next kingdom, the kingdom of Rome, two kings will arise. One will be tough, the other one will be weak, but since they will develop together, the weak king will have some of the strength of the strong one, and people will respect them both. Part of the kingdom will be as strong as iron and the other part will be as weak and as broken as clay. Different nations from the kingdom will intermarry, but as iron does not mix with clay, they will not wholeheartedly mix with one another, and their laws and customs will differ from the laws of the nations they mix with.

[The Book of Creation talks about the remnants of the Roman Empire today, which is divided between USA and the European Union, and includes many different nations. It mentions the diversity today.]

After many years, while the divided kingdom of Rome is still in existence, Creator of heaven will set up his kingdom on earth, which will never be destroyed. This will be a country of Israel, and it will crumble and destroy all other kingdoms. The kingdom of Israel will exist forever. This is the kingdom of Messiah.

The glorious God let you know that, in the end of days; he will set up his kingdom. Just like the stone destroyed and crumbled the statue of gold, copper, iron, silver, and clay, Creator will destroy and crush all other kingdoms. The dream is a prophecy, and it is true because it was revealed to me by the Maker. The Eternal God of Israel neither lies nor changes His mind."

After hearing the explanation, king Nebuchadnezzar fell on his face and bowed himself in front of Daniel to worship him. He offered him a meal-offering, which was a pagan ritual of praise for a pagan deity.

[Daniel has become a God in the eyes of the king of Babylon.]

He said to Daniel, "I can see that your God is the God of Gods and Lord of the Lords. He reveals secrets and he revealed them to you."

The king promptly issued a new decree, ordering to

stop the executions of the wise men in the kingdom. Realizing that Daniel was probably the wisest man in his kingdom, the king Nebuchadnezzar promoted Daniel to the senior government position and gave him many exciting material gifts of clothing, silver, gold and precious stones.

He also gave Daniel ownership of land over all the capital cities of Babylon and appointed him a Chief Officer over all the wise men and princes in Babylon. At the request of Daniel, the king also promoted his three friends to senior positions, over the governing affairs of the capital cities of Babylon. The king made sure that Daniel chambers were prominently located at the king's palace-gate. The king wanted to make sure that Daniel was close-by if he ever needed urgent help.

The cruelty of the pagan world

Five years went by since King Nebuchadnezzar's terrifying dream. The king became extremely arrogant, and had a sudden urge to have an image of gold dedicated to him in a pagan religious ritual. The more kingdoms Babylon conquered; the more arrogant the king became. He started thinking he was invincible. His arrogance and pride grew to the limits that were unheard of. He decided that the whole world had to recognize him as a divine being, and must bow down to his idol.

When people are idol worshipers, some of them start thinking that they are Gods.

Nebuchadnezzar gave an order to his craftsmen to erect his statue. He wanted a statue of gold, which was 104 feet high and 11 foot wide. To make the statue, the gold was melted down from all the gold that Babylon robbed Jerusalem and other kingdoms of. Once ready, the statue was set up in the Valley of Dura, the Capital city of Babylon, on a large vacant lot.

The cruel king chose this area, because of the size, and because this was the place where the Jews and other exiled people were murdered daily after they were brought to Babylon.

At that time, the king sent to gather all the dukes, the chief officers, the governors, the judges, the treasurers, the counselors, the sheriffs and all the rulers of the capital cities to come to the religious dedication ceremony of the image. The dedication was a customary ceremony for the new statue, at the launch of its worship.

If the leaders of the land bow down to king's statue, they will force their subjects to do the same. In our days, the idol worshipers follow the powerful and rich, and bow down to money and materialism.

All the leaders showed up at the appointed time and faced the statue that King Nebuchadnezzar had made for himself. It was an extremely colorful sight because there were thousands of dignitaries in their festive robes. Daniel's friends were there as well, along with some other Jews. Daniel was not at hand. At that time, he was on a king's mission to Alexandria,

Egypt.

As everybody gathered in front of the statue, a loud announcement was made by the messengers, "To all of the people of all the nations and all the languages, we are announcing the command of the king. At the time that you hear a sound of the horn blowing, the harp, the psaltery, the bagpipes and all kinds of music, you shall all fall on the

ground and bow down to the golden image that King Nebuchadnezzar has set up. We warn everyone that whoever doesn't bow down to the statue, will be executed by burning in a fiery furnace."

 By the midday, the sign was finally given, and the whole crowd of people threw themselves to the ground in obedience to the royal decree. That is everyone except three men who remained standing, and they were Daniel's friends Hanniah, Mishael and Azariah. Some other Jews that were participating in the ceremony tried to convince Hananiah, Mishael, and Azariah to obey the king's orders because their faith was not as strong and they did not want to die that day. However, people who worship a real God with conviction, will never bow-down to man-made statue, or other material item.

Five Chaldean men saw that the three Jewish princes did not bow down to Nebuchadnezzar's image. For a while now, they were looking for the opportunity to smear the three Jews. They quickly approached the king and shouted, "May the king live forever! You, king, gave an order that at the sound of music, everyone here should prostate to your image and whoever does not, would be cast into the burning furnace. There are men from the tribe of Judah, who did not bow down to your image. Those are the men, whom you appointed over the government affairs of capital cities of Babylon. They did not follow your order, O king. They do not praise your God, and they do not prostate themselves to the golden image that you had made."

In his extreme wrath, the king had these three Jewish men brought in front of him. The king looked at them angrily, and asked them in the interrogative tone: "Are my decrees void, and desolate, meaningless, and empty in your eyes, O Shadrach, Meshach and Abed-nego? Beware because you are about to make the worst mistake of your lives. Now, I am giving you an order. You will prostate yourselves in front of the image. If you do not bow down to the statue, I shall burn you alive. At that point, we will see if your God saves you from my punishment."

Shadrach, Meshach and Abed-Nego looked the king right in the eye, and Meshach spoke up and called the king by his first name as the sign that he is NOT the god, rather a regular human: "Nebuchadnezzar, God has given us over into your hands as a penalty for not keeping the rules given by the Creator. We serve you devotedly, as you are a king, but not a god. We have only one God and nothing can stop us from worshipping Him alone. You are the king over us, when it comes to taxes, either tax from the crop or head taxes, but if it comes to denying the righteous God in heaven, you have no power over us. You are just a regular person in our eyes, and we do not care about your statue. You beware, because there is God in heavens whom we worship and if he wishes, he can save our bodies from the burning furnace and your hands, O king, He will save us. If he does not save us, let it be known that we will still not praise your God, nor have we willed to prostate to the golden image that you have set up".

[A regular person would say; what is a big deal? I will prostrate to the statue, so my life will be spared. However, for the truly faithful person, it is a matter of principle, and they wouldn't betray God, under any circumstances.]

The king was filled with rage, and his face was red. He shouted loudly and ordered to heat the furnace seven times hotter than usual. "Into the furnace with them, and burn them alive", screamed the enraged Nebuchadnezzar. He summoned 20 mighty warriors, so they can arrest and bind the three Jews. He felt frightened when he realized that they did not fear him.

The three friends were bound in their royal garments and were cast into the fiery furnace. The floor of the furnace was lowered into the fire while the king and a bunch of dignitaries looked in disbelief because they were amazed by the courage of the three Jews. To die in the name of one's God was unheard of in the kingdom, unless it was ordered by the king himself.

The heat of the furnace was so high, and it was heated so excessively that the sparks hit the mighty military men who brought Shadrach, Meshach and Abed-Nego, to the furnace. They caught on fire and burned to death.

The furnace miracle

Hananiah, Mishael and Azariah fell into the fiery roaring furnace bound, as the king watched. Some curious princes, governors, and dukes also gathered around, in order to witness the burning of the insubordinate Jews.

While looking inside the furnace, the king called out in dread and awe: "Behold, I see four men walking in the midst of the fire, and they are unharmed. An angel must've been sent to protect the three faithful Jews from the flames, because of their unwavering faith.

It shows you here that if God finds a merit for you, He will save you from a certain death.

Witnessing the angel saving the Jews, King Nebuchadnezzar approached the gate of the furnace and shouted: "Shadrach, Meshach and Abed-Nego, the servants of the highest God. Step out and join me". The three men realized that a miracle happened, but they still did not dare to come out of the fire from the prospect of totally disrespecting the king, and were waiting for his words. Once the king called them out, they came out of the midst of the fire.

People from all corners of the kingdom witnessed the miracle. They were all astonished that the three men who came out of fire were totally unharmed. Even the smell of fire was not absorbed by their clothing. Every important person in the kingdom of Babylon witnessed the mighty power of God, who saved the three devout Jews from certain death. The king then addressed the other Jews that were present who had earlier bowed down to his idol: "You ought to be ashamed of yourselves! You have such a powerful God, and yet you are so weak as to bow down to my idol..."

In the end of the day, I believe that God had planned the whole incident, so the representatives from the whole kingdom of Babylon, would witness his powers and might.

The king was reminded again that he is nothing but a human being, and he was extremely emotional. Nebuchadnezzar cried out and said: "Blessed be the

God of Shadrach, Meshach and Abed-Nego, who sent his angel and rescued his servants, who trusted him, refusing the command of the king, and risking their lives in order not to worship or prostate themselves to any God except to their own God. I will issue an order to all the people in my kingdom that whoever disrespects the God of Shadrach, Meshach and Abed-Nego, shall be torn to pieces and his house shall be made a dung heap because there is no other God that can perform such miracles."

Then the king went ahead and promoted the three of them. He appointed the three friends in positions of high importance, in the capital city of Babylon. He issued a decree to people of all tongues.

"King Nebuchadnezzar greets all the peoples. May your wealth increase! The signs and wonders of the highest God are immense and mighty. His kingdom is an eternal kingdom, and his dominion is with every generation."

The three Jewish prince's lives were never challenged again. They got married and had children, and lived long and fruitful lives. There is evidence that, at their older age, they returned and lived in the land of Judah.

The King goes mad

A few years went by, and the kingdom of Babylon grew drastically as it defeated more kingdoms and expanded its dominance in the world. With the growth of the kingdom, grew the arrogance of king Nebuchadnezzar, and he became cruel, committing many atrocities and killing many innocent people.

One day he had a disturbing dream. Once he awoke from the dream, he called all of his wise men and told them about it. None of the wise men in Babylon could interpret the dream, until Daniel arrived.

The King was happy to see him and said, "O Belteshazzar, head of the wise men in Babylon, I know that spirit of righteous angels dwells in you, and no secret is hidden from you, and no mystery is denied you. Let me tell you my dream, and you tell me its meaning".

And the king went on telling the dream to Daniel, "In a dream, I found myself looking at the magnificent tree.

Its height was enormous. Its branches were beautiful, and its fruit was plentiful, and it sustained all that were around it. People enjoyed the tree's fruit. Beasts rested in its shade, and birds of the heaven dwelt in its branches. While I was still hypnotized by the beauty of the tree, I saw the angel who never sleeps, descending from heaven. He had a sinister expression, and he cried with all his might,

"Cut down the tree, and cut off its branches. Shake off its branches and scatter its fruit. The birds and the beasts should walk away from it. Leave the main roots in the ground, however."

"That's the dream I had", said the king. "All the wise men of Babylon cannot tell me the meaning, but I know that you can because the spirit of the angels dwells in you."

Daniel looked worried and was silent for a while since his thoughts of the dream interpretation alarmed him. When the king saw his face expression, he spoke up, "Belteshazzar, don't let my dream disturb you."

Daniel raised his eyes to heaven and said in Hebrew: "My God, may this dream be fulfilled upon this enemy of yours". He turned to the king and said: "The tree in the dream was you, for you have become renowned, and your cruelty and evil deeds reached the heavens. The words of the angel mean that you, O king, will be punished, you will lose your mind and will be banished from the humanity and will stay with the beasts for seven years. You'll get a seven-year penalty because you destroyed the High Temple in Jerusalem, which took seven years to build. Your dwelling will be with the beasts of the field, until you understand that the Highest God is the ruler over the kingdom of men, not you, and He is the one that sets up kings or removes kings as he wishes. He said to leave the roots of the tree because the kingdom will remain to be yours and you will be restored to your power when you know that the kingdom of heaven rules over the dominion of men."

Although King Nebuchadnezzar was an instrument of God, for his bad deeds he had to receive very harsh punishment.

"I shall advice you to increase your charity and show mercy to poor Jews and other peoples whom you have exiled from their land. Remove your sins and wickedness, by showing mercy to those people in exile, and feed them to allow them to have a dignified life. Pray and ask for forgiveness for your evil deeds, so that God forgives you and gives you peace".

The king listened to Daniel's advice, and issued an order to feed poor exiles who had difficulty to support their families honorably. The country opened its storehouses and started feeding the poor.

At the end of 12 month, the king was walking in the palace when he heard noises of commotion outside the palace. He asked his servants, "What is this sound of the crowd in my ears?" The servants answered that those were the poor people, who came at the arranged time, to get food. At that point, the king raised his voice and said, "Is not the dominant Babylon that I have built with the strength of my power and for the honor of my glory? If I have to waste my storehouses on these people, how can I afford to stay glorious? From now on, I shall not feed them."

After uttering those arrogant words, the king heard a voice from heaven above which said, "To you, they said, 'O king Nebuchadnezzar, that your kingdom has turned away from you. From men, they will banish you, and you will be dwelling with the beasts until seven years will pass, and until you know that the Highest God rules over the kingdom of men, and to whom he wishes, he gives it".

At that moment the king lost his mind and was banished from the men-kind. He ate grass like cattle, and his body was drenched with the dew of the heavens until his hair grew like the feathers of the eagles and his nails grew like the claws of the birds.

At the end of his days, after seven years, Nebuchadnezzar raised his eyes to heavens and blessed the Almighty. As his sanity was restored, he said, "My understanding was restored to me, and I worship and glorify the God who lives forever and whose dominion is an everlasting dominion, and whose kingdom lasts for every generation. No one can stop His hand and challenge Him. Now, I,

Nebuchadnezzar, praise and exalt and glorify the king of heaven, whose works are all true and whose ways are just, and who can humble those who walk with arrogance."

At that time, the king was restored to his kingship and ruled the kingdom until the end of his days. After his death, his son, Evil-Merodach reined the kingdom for 23 years. After his death, his younger brother, Belshazzar has become the king of Babylon.

The evil empire

Years went by, and Daniel was already in his 40's. His life in the kingdom of Babylon was extremely prosperous and secure. He held extremely powerful government positions and had a significant influence over government, social, religious and financial affairs in the kingdom. Daniel had everything anyone could wish for - land, treasures, and other material possessions. Regardless, he was still longing for his family and the beautiful country of Judah. He was ready to trade all the riches and power just to be with his family again. He was wondering if his parents were still alive.

 This revelation happened in the kingdom of Babylon, 23 years after king Nebuchadnezzar's death. In the first year of King Belshazzar reign, Daniel had a revelation at night, in a form of a dream. In the revelation, Daniel was transformed to a different reality, and found himself standing by the shore of the Mediterranean Sea. There was eerie quietness in the air. All of a sudden, mysterious and strong winds came from all the directions of the world and stirred up the magnificent sea. Large waves started crashing on the shore. Daniel took a few steps away, and while looking anxiously at the sea, he saw four gigantic beasts emerging out of water one by one. It was a breathtaking sight of epic proportions because the beasts were like no other beasts in the world. Daniel wondered what it all meant.

As the beasts slowly emerged from the sea, Daniel saw a group of men assembling close by. They were listening to another man on a podium. He was issuing what sounded like a verdict. Daniel approached the group, and greeted one of the men who were standing. He asked him what was going on, and what he was witnessing.

The man greeted him back, and said, "You are witnessing a revelation for the events which will occur in a very distant future. You are here because you were chosen by the righteous God, to receive this revelation. God wants you to understand what the fate of the Jewish people in the distant future will be. These four beasts are representations of the kingdoms that will happen in the future. The righteous

Jews, who observe the Commandments, will take the land from the fourth one, forever and to all eternity."

At that moment, Daniel realized that although this looked like a place on earth, it was not. He understood that he was transformed to the place which was not of this earth, to a different realm. Looking closely at the men around him, he noticed that the "men" were not men at all because they had no joints in their hands and legs. He felt both humbled and frightened once he realized that he was in the company of angels.

Daniel looked at the first beast with curiosity. The beast looked like a huge lion, and it had wings of an eagle. As the creature was coming out of the sea, an unseen hand plunked its wings out, took out its heart, and replaced it with the human heart.

The second beast came out of the water and stood on the other beast's right. It looked like a giant bear. There were three ribs in its mouth, and it kept chewing them, and spitting them out. Then it would pick them off the ground and put them in its mouth again.

The third creature looked like a spotted leopard. It had four heads and four wings of a bird on its back.

Daniel abruptly awoke from the dream and could not forget the sight. He tried to concentrate on his government work all day, but could not forget the visions of the previous night.

The following night Daniel had another revelation. The prophecy was a continuity of the dream he had the night before. Daniel found himself standing among the angels, next to the stormy sea, watching the fourth beast emerging from the water. It was a terrible beast. It was bigger than an elephant and it looked remarkably frightening and strong. The creature had large iron teeth, and it was devouring everything around it, crushing everything in its mouth. On its head, there were ten horns. Suddenly, another little horn grew on its head in place of three horns. Daniel was shocked because the little horn had human eyes and a mouth that was speaking against God arrogantly!

The angel next to him waited a few moments until Daniel recollected himself, and then explained the revelation, "The first creature that emerged from the sea last night symbolized the kingdom of Babylon that is in existence right now. The beast had wings of an eagle to symbolize that it's in power right now. Its wings were plunked out, which is an allusion of its downfall. A heart of a mortal man was given to it, as an expression of weakness. It means that kingdom of Babylon will come to an end and will forever disappear from this earth"

"The second beast represents the kingdom of Persia, which will reign after the kingdom of Babylon. It looked like a bear because the Persians are barbaric like a bear; they eat and drink like a bear, and wrap themselves in animal skin. The bear stood to the side, indicating that when the kingdom of Babylon terminates, Persia will wait for one year, when kingdom of Media will reign. There were three ribs in the creature's mouth, symbolizing the three kings who will emerge from Persia - Cyrus, Ahasuerus, and Darius."

"The third beast represents the kingdom of Antiochus the Greek that will emerge after Persia. It is spotted because the Greeks will be inconsistent and will have different rules and regulations in the different provinces of the kingdom. It had four heads and four wings of a bird on its back, and control of the earth will be given to it. The leopard's four heads are the four rulers who will arise after Alexander Macedon's death."

Daniel tried to understand. He felt overwhelmed by the epic and artistic display in front of him. The angel waited a moment, and proceeded with the explanation; "The last beast is a kingdom of Rome, which will emerge after the kingdom of Greeks. It had ten horns, to symbolizing the ten kings that will climb to the throne. The 11th little horn,

which grew on its head, and three first horns were plunked out of it, symbolizes Titus Vespasian. The little horn had human eyes and a mouth that was speaking highly arrogantly because Titus will be an incarnation of evil. He will curse and rebuke God, and will destroy the Temple in Jerusalem."

Suddenly, the angel was silent as Daniel observed that two magnificent royal thrones appeared nearby.

An angel announced in a loud voice, "God has arrived to proclaim the final judgment for the world". The angel next to Daniel explained: "One throne is for judging the different nations for their transgressions, and the other is for the charity of Israel. On that throne, God will remove all the inequities of the Jews and the other people, who will still hold faith, and observe the commandments till the end."

We learn that people, who will still possess faith till the end of the world, will be purified from their iniquities in the end by God himself. That means that God will remove the evil inclination from them.

Daniel was shocked and frozen, as he saw that suddenly one of the thrones was occupied. Creator was seated on the throne. Daniel had to cover his eyes, because of an intense light that was emanating from Creator. The throne was made of sparks of fire; it had wheels, which were a burning fire.

River of fire was flowing and emerging from before him. Thousands and thousands of angels assembled around him and served him. There were thousands of angels singing for Him. His robes were as white as snow, and His hair was white like pure linen.

It wants to show us here that God is the king of kings, and has more servants than all the kings combined.

An angel made a loud announcement, "Justice is established before God, and the records are open! These are the records of transgressions and the evil deeds that different nations of the world committed."

Daniel was stunned and could not move. He felt mortified in the presence of God. He watched hypnotized that from the sound of the arrogant words from the mouth of the small horn, on the head of the fourth beast, the wrath of God was aroused, and He ordered to slay the beast. The dreadful beast was slain by the angels, and its body was burned in the flame of fire. "That will be the destiny of the kingdom of Rome in the end of days," said the angel. "As for the other kingdoms, their dominion of the earth was taken away from them, by heaven. None of them will be powerful again to rule the earth. They were given an extension of life to live until a set day in the future, when the last war of Gog and Magog will happen."

Daniel tried to follow through. He was flooded with awe and delights that God found him to be significant enough to be shown what will happen in the future. As he was taking the information in, suddenly, from the clouds, a person appeared. He was immediately greeted by the angels, and was brought in front of God, who was still sitting, and judging other nations.

Angel said, "That man is the Messiah. He will be a leader in the End of the World. God will give him power, glory and the dominion over all the nations. His kingdom will never be removed."

Daniel was shaken up. He wanted to know more in order to understand the prophecy, and he started asking questions. He wanted to know more about the fourth beast, which was different from all the other ones, and was exceedingly dreadful. About the one that had iron teeth and crushed everything in its mouth into fine powder. Daniel also wanted to know more about the horns on its head, and the last one that came up, and the three first horns that fell before it.

The angel answered: "This horn is the Roman King

Titus. He will lead his army, waging war with the righteous Israel and will overwhelm them. He will succeed in oppressing them for many years until God comes and takes revenge for the righteous Jews, and the time comes when the Jews inherit the kingdom."

"The ten horns that sprout from the fourth beast's head represent ten kings in the empire. The last king that will arise after them will be different from the first and will humble three kings. That is Titus. This king will change the decree of three former kings, and convert the land to worship the pagan "god". He will speak words against God and will oppress the Jews. He will make plans to cause them to betray God, and break all of their Jewish commandments, rituals, and laws. For that purpose, he will create a pagan religion. The righteous Jews will be delivered into his hand because of their transgressions, until a time, two times and half a time."

[The Book of Creation talks about Christianity.]

And then the angel warned him, "And you, Daniel, close up the words and seal. The set time for the end of days is hidden. Do not tell anyone about it. When that day arrives, the judgment shall be established before God, and God will remove the control and the power of the Roman kingdom."

"The kingdom and authority and the significance of the kingdoms under all the heavens will be given to the people of the righteous Jews, and the people who practice the Commandments. That kingdom will be an everlasting kingdom. All the dominions will serve it and obey it forever and ever."

Daniel awoke from the revelation. He hid all that he saw in his mind for now. The whole prophecy terrified him and troubled him. He realized that the second Temple is destined to be destroyed as well, and the people of Israel had many troubles and tribulations ahead, for many years to come.

The nation of Israel

Another year went by. It was daytime, and Daniel was alone, working in his chamber. Suddenly, he felt tired and fell asleep. Once he woke up, he found himself alone on the edge of the capital city of Shushan, which was located in the province of Elam. To the east there was a river of Ulai, and on the other side he could see the city. He had a strange feeling that something mysterious was going on, because of the silence in the air. He could hear the river, but he could not hear a bird singing, or wind blowing.

 As he lifted his eyes to look around, he saw a big beautiful ram standing next to the river, about 100 feet away from him. Daniel had a feeling that the ram could not see him. As Daniel focused his attention on the ram, he observed two large horns growing on its head. One horn was smaller than the other one.

All of a sudden, different beasts came to attack it from the south and from the north. First came a large bull, charging from the south. The ram gored it and killed it immediately. Then, a lion came charging from the north. After a short battle, the ram gored it and crushed it. The ram kept on fighting different animals that were charging from different directions, and killed every one of them. No animal or beast could stand in front of it, and manage to survive.

He looked around and saw a large male goat charging from the west, towards the ram. It had a huge horn between its eyes. The goat was running so fast that its feet were not touching the ground. It seemed as if he were skipping in the air while running.

 The goat ran to the ram with passionate fury and attacked it. It was a magnificent fight. No matter how hard the ram fought, it was defeated, and lost both of its horns. The goat struck it on its side and cast it to the ground. He stood on it, crushed it with its feet and flattened it. The ram had no chance to survive, and died.

[Note that the Book of Creation shows different nations as beasts, because they are pagan.]

Daniel kept on looking at the goat with a growing curiosity. He was hypnotized by its magnificent appearance. There was no other animal left to fight it.

It cleaned and beautified itself after the fight and grew in size, to become a gigantic beast. Within next five minutes, as the goat grew in size, the large horn broke, and instead of it, four smaller horns sprouted. Each of those four horns faced to the different directions of the earth.

Daniel observed that immediately, out of one of those four horns, emerged a small horn that grew larger and larger to the direction of Egypt and to the direction of the coveted land of Israel. The horn kept on growing until it reached the sky. As it grew ever larger, it reached the stars and covered many of them with its shadow.

[The Book of Creation compares the righteous Jews to stars.]

Daniel was stunned and wondered what it all meant. As he watched the horn grow, he heard a man's voice reading a verdict out of nowhere. The verdict read the following,

"A verdict was issued from God to punish the Jews for their transgressions and inequities. For the duration of this verdict, they will experience enormous suffering and misery, and their prayers in the Temple will not be answered."

Another voice asked the man who was issuing the verdict, "How long is God's verdict for the Jews to be punished, pagan rule to continue, and the disgrace of the Temple to be allowed?"

[Creator believes in a collective punishment. Although the bad Jews were the ones, who helped Titus to create Christianity, He punished all the Jews. The punishment is thousands of years of test of faith.]

The first voice answered: "Evening and morning, two thousand and three hundred. It is many lifetimes until they pass the test. However, the Jews who are already righteous, and follow the commandments, will be spared".

If you die righteous and innocent, you don't come back to this earth to suffer further. Creator will keep your soul with him, until the end of days.

Daniel knew that he was experiencing some momentous and terrible revelation about the faith of his people, but was struggling to understand exactly what was going on. As he was looking around to see where the voices were coming from, a loud voice came from the midst of the river, which said, "Gabriel, explain this man what this revelation is about."

Out of nowhere, a man appeared. He was wearing warrior robes. As the man spoke, Daniel's knees gave up, and he fell on the ground.

The stranger helped Daniel to get on his feet and addressed him, "Daniel, do not be afraid. I am angel Gabriel. God sent me to you. The revelation refers to time that is needed for God's fury at your people to end. It will happen many years from now, at the End of Days. I also want you to know about all the significant events, which will take place from now until the time of the end."

"The apparition is a metaphor. In the apparition, the ram with two horns represents kings of Media and Persia, the two nations that will rule in the future."

"The goat represents the kingdom of Greece, and the humongous horn between his eyes, is the first king

Alexander Macedon. The same large horn that was broken, in whose stead stood four smaller horns, represents four different Alexander Macedon's family members, but not his children. They will rule after his death. However, none of these four kings will be as strong as Alexander Macedon, and none of the four will be able to rule the whole earth. "

Alexander Macedon knew that none of his family members were as tough as him, to rule the whole kingdom, so he divided it between four of them.

"At the end of their kingdoms, a shameless king will arise. He will understand mysteries, riddles, and will be a professional liar. This is King Titus. He will be the incarnation of pure evil. It will be a tough time for Israel. In that era, the second Temple in Jerusalem will be built, and many Jews in those days will be wicked people and idol worshipers."

Daniel was hypnotized by the voice of the angel. He listened to every word very carefully. The angel paused for a moment, and kept explaining.

"Titus' power will be great, but not through the

strength of his armies, rather through his sweet talk, lies and diplomacy. He will destroy many mighty nations, including many righteous Jews, who believe in Creation. Through his wit, deceit, and lies, wherever he will turn, he will succeed. As time goes on, his arrogance will grow larger, and he will become even a bolder liar. He will form peace treaty with many nations and earn their trust. However, shortly thereafter he will betray and destroy them."

[We learn here that unlike the primitive concept of evil, the evil doesn't come to you to attack you. It comes as a friend to earn your trust, and once you lower your guard, it destroys you.]

"Titus will make a peace treaty with princes of Israel, to lead them believe that he comes in peace. Later he will betray them and destroy them as well. He will repeatedly rebuke God and will talk blasphemously about His kingdom. As a punishment for his terrible actions, he will die in torture dishonorably, in the most humiliating way. The weakest of the creatures, a mosquito, will enter his nose and give him a deadly illness. The vision of the evening and morning, which you heard in the previous revelation, is true. Do not explain this revelation. Close it up in your mind, for it will come true in many years from now."

Immediately after the angel finished the sentence, Daniel awoke in his chamber with a feeling of restlessness. He kept busy, but could not forget the revelation and was extremely depressed about it. He restrained himself before the princes and the people, and nobody realized what was going on in his mind.

The fall of Babylonian

In the second year of Belshazzar's reign, the king came back after a great battle with king Darius the Mede and King Cyrus of Persia. Since he was victorious in that battle, he invited 1000 of his dignitaries to a great feast to celebrate the victory. Those dignitaries included the local governors, viziers, army generals, and supernatural priests. Daniel was not invited.

The king was in a good mood and drank lots of wine. It was a marvelous feast. Beautiful women danced to the music, and the best food in the kingdom was served.

In his drunkenness, the king ordered to bring the golden and silver vessels that his father, king Nebuchadnezzar, robbed from Jerusalem's Temple, so he and his guests could drink wine from them. The vessels were brought and all of the people at the feast started drinking from them. While drinking, they blessed the pagan Gods of gold, silver, iron, wood and stone.

Suddenly, to the amazement of everyone at the feast, a human hand emerged from nowhere, and started writing on the wall. The king was very frightened. His knees shook from fear. He was so startled that he urinated himself.

The king cried out loud to bring in the Necromancers, the Chaldeans and the astrologers to interpret the writing on the wall. Once the wise men appeared, he promised those riches and a third of the kingdom if they could interpret the writing on the wall. The wise men tried to interpret the writing, but none of them could figure it out.

At that point, the king was even more frightened. All the dignitaries who were present were extremely confused. They did not know what to do with themselves. The music stopped playing, and everyone was looking at each other, wondering what was going to happen next. Eventually, after minutes of silence, the queen entered the banquet hall and approached the king. She said to him quietly, "May the king live forever! Do not let your thoughts frighten you. There is a man in your kingdom with the spirit of angels. Your father, king Nebuchadnezzar appointed him as a prince of the Necromancers, the Astrologers, the Chaldeans and the Demonologists. He interpreted your father's dreams, and he can interpret the writing on the wall. His name is Daniel, whom your father called Belteshazzar."

The king immediately ordered to bring in Daniel, and within a half an hour, he was there. The king asked him, "Are you Daniel, whom my father brought from the kingdom of Judah as an exile? I heard that the spirit of angels is in you, and you are of superior wisdom. If you can read the writing on the wall, and interpret it, you shall wear purple clothing, like the highest nobles, and wear a golden chain on your neck, and you shall rule the third of my kingdom"

Daniel replied, "Keep your gifts, or give them to someone else because I do not need them. I shall read the writing for the king, and I shall let him know the interpretation."

He took a deep breath and continued, "You are the king because the highest God gave your father,

Nebuchadnezzar, the kingdom, greatness, honor and glory. Because of all the greatness God gave your father, all the nations and people feared him. Whomever he wished, he would slay, and whomever he wished, he would bless; whomever he wished, he would promote, and whomever he wished he would humble. When his mind became too dark and wicked, your father was thrown off the royal throne. At that point, he was banished from the mankind, and his mind was just like that of beasts, and his dwelling was with the wild asses. He ate grass like the cattle, and his body was drenched in dew of the heavens until he realized that the highest God rules over the kingdom of men, and whomever he wishes, he sets upon it." Daniel paused for a few seconds and then continued,

"But you, Belshazzar, did not humble your mind in view of the fact that you know all this, and you still did not respect the God. You dared to bring vessels from the house of the Lord in heavens, and you, your dignitaries, your queen and your concubines drank wine from them. You praised the idol gods of silver, gold, copper, iron, wood and stone, which you neither see, nor hear, nor know, but the Creator who has your soul in his hands, you forgot to praise. "

[The Book of Creation shows here that although God already knows that the wicked will transgress, He always hopes that he/she will change for better.]

"The hand was sent forth to inscribe this writing: MENE TEKEIL UFARSIN, which means,

MENE: God has counted the end of the allotted time for the kingdom of your father and his seed and has brought it to an end. The allotted time for the kingdom of Babylon ended.

TEKEIL: You were weighed on the scale and found wanting of all righteousness.

UFARSIN: Your kingdom has been broken up to two parts. One has been given to Media and the other one to Persia."

King Belshazzar was terribly scared and distraught. Nevertheless he gave Daniel the rewards he promised.

That very night, Belshazzar's enemies returned,

waged war on the city, and this time captured it. King Belshazzar was assassinated, and Darius the Mede received the kingdom at the age of 62. King Darius, who was king Nebuchadnezzar's adversary, was born 62 years earlier, exactly when king Nebuchadnezzar conquered Judah, deposed king Jehoiakim, and entered and disrespected the High Temple in Jerusalem.

The day that king Nebuchadnezzar destroyed the Temple in Jerusalem, was the day that God judged him and sentenced his son to die by the hand of his adversary, King Darius, who was born in that day, 62 years earlier. Now you understand that when you make a move, God makes his move to sentence you.

The Lion's den miracle

Once King Darius the Mede began his rule, he immediately appointed 120 governors to help him govern the entire kingdom. Each one was in charge of a province, and in charge over them the king appointed 3 viziers, one of which was Daniel.

Over a short time of a few months, Daniel surpassed the other 2 viziers in his wisdom and positive spirit. The king started liking him and trusting him. At that point, king Darius made up his mind to appoint him to be in charge over the entire kingdom, and the other viziers.

The other viziers and the governors were extremely jealous over Daniel's promotion and success. They started looking for some faults with Daniel in order to accuse him in something, so they could report him to the king. They could not find anything against him because Daniel was trustworthy and honest with no faults. Finally, these wise men decided to use Daniel's love of God against him. Twenty of them gathered and went to the king, and told him, "King Darius, may you live forever! To preserve the king's law and strengthen your authority since you have just ascended to the throne, and you are a foreigner, you are in need of support. We have decided, O King, that all the people of the land should not worship any god other than you for thirty days. Let's issue a decree that whoever breaks the order should be cast into a lions' den. This way people will recognize that you are a powerful king. O King, please issue a decree and inscribe a writ that this law cannot be amended, like the law of Media and Persia, which will not be repealed." Since the whole world was practicing idol worship, and this was a way to boost his power, king Darius liked the idea. He inscribed a writ and a decree that, for thirty days, nobody could worship any god, but him.

Daniel was one of the first people to find out about the new decree because he was in a high government position. His business was to know everything significant that happened in the kingdom. He was a bit frustrated because he had a feeling that some Chaldean men were plotting against him. However, since he was well aware that he was living in a foreign land, which was a pagan world, he was not surprised.

Although the new decree prohibited a worship of any god for 30 days, Daniel was not about to betray his faith. He had conviction like no one else. He felt that his duty was to follow the command of God, no matter what. The fear of death was never a factor in his decisions. He would prefer death over breaking God's laws.

After he finished his daily duties that day, he came home, and before the evening meal, he went to the upper floor of his house to pray. Daniel went to the room, with the windows facing Jerusalem, and prayed to God as he did every day. He thanked Him for safety and good fortune. Since the windows of the room were open, his enemies saw him praying to his God. Right away those spies went to the king to inform him that Daniel broke his decree by praying to his God.

Here again, you see that the faithful person doesn't care about king's decrees or laws. For Daniel and other faithful people, God and His laws are above any human law!

The king was highly displeased when he heard this news, even though Daniel was a highly trusted man to him, and his death would be painful to him. He told the wise men, who informed him about Daniel that he did not believe them and wanted more proof. He told them that he would send his own people to spy on Daniel, to see if Daniel would pray to his God again at sunrise. Once the morning arrived, and other witnesses saw Daniel praying to his God, the king had no choice left but to order to cast Daniel into the lions' den.

Once Daniel was brought in front of him for judgment, king Darius said, "May your God, whom you serve regularly, save you." Daniel thanked the king for his efforts. He was not scared, and decided to trust himself in the hands of Creator. He was totally convinced that if Creator would find a reason to keep him alive, no harm will come to him.

With the king's supervision, Daniel was placed in the lions' den, with 100 hungry lions. The lions were an integral part of the Median culture and were used regularly for the king's amusement, as well as for other purposes.

The opening of the pit was sealed with a large stone, to prevent Daniel's escape. The king went ahead and sealed the pit's opening with his signed seal, to make sure that no other man could open the lions' den and hurt Daniel by stoning him. Then the King turned to the people around him and said: "It is painful for me to do this, but I have no choice. From the lions, I cannot save him, but I shall be careful with him that no man can hurt him, so if the miracle comes, and he lives, let it happen."

The king was restless and could not eat or drink that day. He could not fall asleep for a long time. He tossed and turned all night. He was seriously worried about Daniel and got up two hours earlier than usual, at the break of dawn. He immediately went to the pit to check on Daniel. When he approached the lions' pit, he called out with the sad voice, "Daniel, the servant of the living God, the God whom you worship regularly, did He save you from death?" Daniel immediately answered from the pit, "May the king live forever! My God sent his angel, who closed the mouths of the lions, and they did not hurt me. God has found virtue in me before him and before you, because O king, I have done no wrong." Turns out that the whole day and night Daniel was in the lions' den, the lions did not exhibit any form of aggressiveness, as if Daniel was never there.

Here we learn that if you are a pure person like Daniel, no harm will ever come to you.

The king was relieved. He ordered Daniel out of the pit. The king and his court were totally astonished that no injuries were found on Daniel. There was not a single scratch on his body. Everyone realized that Daniel was saved because he totally and undoubtedly believed in his God.

So, king Darius decided that people, who plotted against Daniel, deserved an extremely harsh punishment. For the king, Daniel was one of the most influential people in the entire kingdom for his talents, honesty and loyalty. He realized that those 20 wise men conspired to have Daniel killed. He decided to punish the conspirators with the same medicine that

Daniel was given. He issued an order to arrest them along with their family members. The accusers and their families were thrown into the lions' pit and did not even reach the bottom of the pit before they were torn apart by the lions.

King Darius was so impressed with the events, that the following day he issued an order through the whole kingdom, in all the 50 languages of people. The order read the following:

"I wish you all peace! I issued an order in the entire dominion of my kingdom that everyone should be awestricken before God of Daniel, for He is a living God, who exists forever. His kingdom will not be ever destroyed. He saves and rescues and performs signs and wonders in heaven and on earth."

We learn here that although God could make sure that those slanderous Chaldeans wouldn't hurt Daniel, He prefers the drama, to instill fear and respect into pagans. This way God hopes that one's witnessing His power and might, some of them might convert to Judaism, as an example of Moses' father-in-law.

Jerusalem's destruction

This following revelation took place in the first year of reign of king Darius, the son of Ahasuerus of the seed of Media, who was crowned over the kingdom of Chaldeans, which was called the kingdom of Babylon earlier.

Daniel was doing his job as a chief vizier of the whole kingdom, overlooking the political, social, and religious affairs of the whole kingdom. He constantly tried to keep busy, because he could not seat idle. He constantly kept thinking about the revelations of the end of days.

He felt both humbled and proud that God found him worthy enough to give him the most significant revelations of the mankind. Daniel understood principally, what God had in mind for people of Israel, and the rest of the nations. He could not get the thought out of his mind, and truly wanted to know when it would happen.

It truly bothered him that there were so many unscrupulous Jews among them, who despite to all the wonders and miracles that Creator performed, reverted to idol worship and paganism, and abandoned their fellow Jews. Daniel was aware of the fact that the Prophet Jeremiah had the end of the days revealed to him, after the destruction of Jerusalem. One day, he decided to beg the Lord to give him more information about the end of days.

After thinking for a while, Daniel crafted a distinctive prayer. That same afternoon, he read the prayer out loud:

"Please, O Lord, O great and awesome Creator, who keeps the covenant and shines His light upon those who love Him and keep His commandments. We have sinned and have dealt iniquitously. We have dealt wickedly and have rebelled, turning away from your commandments and your ordinances. We did not obey your servants, the prophets, who spoke in your name to our kings, our princes, and our forefathers, and to all the people in the land. To you, O Lord is the righteousness, and to us is the shamefacedness as of this day, to the people of Judah, to the inhabitants of Jerusalem, and to all Israel both near and far, in all the lands to which you have driven them for the treachery that they have perpetrated toward you. "

"O Lord, to us is shamefacedness, to our kings, to our princes, and to our forefathers, who transgressed against you. We ask you for mercy and pardon, for we have rebelled against you. We admit that we did not follow your teachings and your voice, which you placed before us by your servants, the prophets. Israel has transgressed your teaching, turning away, not heeding your voice, and the curse and great evil have befallen upon us as it is written in the Law of Moses, which we transgressed against. Please remove your wrath and your anger from us, for because our transgressions and iniquities of our forefathers, Jerusalem and your people have become a mockery to all those surrounding us."

While Daniel was still praying, angel Gabriel, whom Daniel saw in a previous vision, in the days of King Belshazzar, swiftly approached him. He landed next to Daniel, and said,

"Daniel, I came here to enable you to understand the future events. An order came from God Himself. Since you are pure, He wants you to understand the destiny of people of Israel and the destiny of all the other nations. Now, pay attention and make sure that you understand what I am about to say."

It teaches us here, that the prayers of a pure and innocent person are always heard by God.

"Four hundred and ninety years of exile were ruled upon your people and the city of the Temple. This will terminate the transgression and will end the transgression. Than the Temple will be destroyed the second time so that Israel should receive their complete retribution in the exile of Titus and suppression. At that time, their transgressions should stop, their punishments end, and their iniquities atoned, in order to bring eternal justice upon them and to give them the Holy of the Holies, The Ark of Covenant, the altars, and the vessels, which they will bring to them through king Messiah."

And as Daniel listened attentively, the angel continued, "And you should know from the information that I am giving you, how to restore and build Jerusalem. Time will be given from the day of the destruction until the coming of anointed king, King Cyrus, king of Persia; about whom God said that he would return and build His city. At that time, the city, its streets, and walls to protect it, will be built. This will happen in troubled times because, in those times, the Persians and Heathens will burden your people under a heavy bondage."

The Book of Creation teaches us here that the moment that the first temple was destroyed by the Babylonians, Creator already made His move to have a Persian king come in the future, to rebuild it. The plans of God are like those of the most sophisticated chess grandmaster. When his adversaries make a move in their human mortal way, He counters them with His move, which goes on for generations.

"And after 434 years from now, the anointed king Agrippa of Judah will be slain, and the city and the Temple will be destroyed by a conquering monarch, Titus, and his armies. His [Titus] end will be damnation and destruction in the future through the

Messiah, and until the end of the wars of Gog the city of Jerusalem will exist."

Here another concrete proof of God for you! The Book of Creation makes a statement 2500 years ago, that Jerusalem will always exist. There is no other city in the world that existed for even 1000 years.

"King Titus will make a treaty with princes of Israel at first and promise them peace for seven years, but within those seven years, he will break his promise. He will put an end to the ritual meal sacrifice to God in the Temple, and among the atrocities, he will place a dumb statue at the altar of the temple. The ruling of disgrace will endure until the set time, when extermination and destruction will befall the dumb pagan god, and its worshippers, in the days of King Messiah. The final judgment and sentencing of each individual, good or bad, will come at the end of days. That is when HELL will be established."

"Farewell, Daniel, and write everything down. When the right time comes, I will return again and complete the information about the end of days ", said the angel and vanished into the thin air.

Daniel was left wondering about the faith of the Jewish people. A complete picture about the future started emerging in his mind. He was wondering why Jewish people were getting punished so hard for their actions.

Daniel prospered in the time of rule of king Darius and was never challenged again. King Darius of Mede reigned for only one year before he died in a battle. Upon his death, his son in law, Cyrus of Persia was crowned as a king. The kingdom of Media was no more, and kingdom of Persia was established.

End of the World prophecy

Years went by and Daniel was already 88 years old. He was very rich and lived a comfortable life. Since he was still living in the kingdom of Persia, he was not completely happy. He mourned the destruction of the Temple for twenty one years. He fasted and did not eat bread and meat or drank wine. He prayed twice daily, and asked for forgiveness from God for the transgressions committed by the Jewish people. He also prayed for the restoration of the Temple and the kingdom of Judah. As angel Gabriel predicted 40 years earlier, King Cyrus of Persia started rebuilding the Temple, but the work was progressing slowly.

It was year 529BC. On the 24th day of the month of Nisan, Daniel was standing on the banks of the majestic river Tigris, near the capital city of Pasargadae, with three of his friends. He was taking a walk after a short illness. Looking at the river, he saw a strange vision. It looked like there was a man suspended in the air in the middle of the river over the water. He was wearing beautiful white cloths of linen, and a belt of gold. The belt was studded with clusters of precious pearls. His body was three times larger than of a regular human. His face was bright as a lightning bolt, and his eyes were shining like burning fire. His arms and legs looked like they were made out of refined shiny copper. When the apparition spoke, the sound of his voice sounded like a sound of a legion. The three friends, who were with Daniel, were not able to see him. However, they felt that something scary was going on, and fled into the hiding.

The person cannot see some supernatural beings, but his guardian angel can. Therefore, he still feels scared.

The apparition was so frightful that Daniel trembled. As he noticed that his friends left him, he felt weakness creeping into his knees, and he could not gather up strength. When he heard the frightful voice of the apparition talking to him, he lost consciousness and fell on the ground. Moments later, when he opened his eyes, he saw that he was not alone. Archangel Gabriel, whom he knew from the previous revelation years earlier, was gently shaking him up to wake him. The angel smiled to Daniel, and helped him get up on his feet. He said in a friendly voice, "Daniel, man of desirable qualities, stand upright and listen to my words carefully. Because of your prayers, I was allowed to come through the curtain to space and time, because of you. God and his dwelling are right here, but in a different dimension."

Daniel forced himself to smile back. He glanced at the river and noticed that the frightful apparition was still there. The angel continued talking in a calm voice, "Do not be scared Daniel. That is Archangel Michael over the water. God allowed him to accompany me on this mission. Since the first day you started fasting and setting your prayers before your God, you were heard, and God decided to send us. My previous mission was in Gods Court of Justice. I was appointed as a defendant for the Jewish people against the Archangel of Persia. He was pleading for an extension of time for the kingdom of Persia, in order to enable them to suppress the

Jews. It took me 21 days to win the case. Archangel Michael is particularly concerned with the welfare of your people, and assisted me in that matter. I came to you in order to enable you to understand what has not yet been told to you in previous revelations. Creator wants you to know that He has already issued the final judgment, concerning the timing of the End of Days, fate of this world, and fate of the Jewish people."

Daniel was speechless. His whole body trembled. The experience was overwhelming for him. The angel touched his lips, and magically Daniel was able to talk again. He managed to say "As a servant of my Lord, I am not able to speak because the strength will not stay in me." The angel touched Daniel on the shoulder and said, "Fear not, man of desirable qualities; peace be upon you. Be strong and be strong." With these words, Daniel gained more strength and said, "Let my Lord speak, for you have strengthened me."

The angel said, "After I leave you, I have to return to Gods Court of Justice, to wrap up the case with the archangel of Persia. I won that case, but I lost another, against the archangel of Greece. In that case, God has issued a hard sentence against the Jews. Although Israel is subjugated by the kings of Persia these days, they will not be burdened heavily. However, the king of heathens, Antiochus, will lay a heavy yoke upon them. Indeed I shall tell you that God has issued a difficult verdict against your people. However, Archangel Michael is extremely concerned with the verdict and hopes to change His mind, in order to lighten it."

Archangel Michael is a prince angel of the Jews.

[Creator knew that the Jews had many wicked among them, so He decided to administer a more terrible test of faith, through Greek bondage, to see who will remain with faith.]

Daniel was confused. He realized that the Jewish people were destined for many years of suffering. Angel Gabriel saw how confused and distraught Daniel was, and immediately said with the comforting voice, "You have got to be strong, Daniel, because my time is limited. Concentrate and listen carefully, because now I will tell you the rest of the prophecy."

"After King Cyrus I, three more kings will arise in Persia - Cyrus, Cambyses and Ahasuerus, and the forth one, king Darius, will become extremely powerful and wealthy. He will decide to raise his entire kingdom to wage war against the kingdom of Heathens [Greece]. At the meantime, in Greece, a powerful king will arise, Alexander Macedon. He will slay king Darius, defeat the Persians and enslave them."

"When Alexander Macedon reaches the height of his strength, his kingdom will be broken because he will die. Before his death, he will divide his kingdom between his 4 family members, but not his children. Those four kingdoms will rule the four directions of heaven. They will not be as strong as Alexander Macedon's kingdom, and none of them will be able to rule over the whole earth."

"The king that will reign in the south, in the kingdom of Egypt, will be a stronger leader than the king who rules in the north, in the kingdom of Greece. After a few years, they will make a compromise of peace between them and a daughter of the king of Egypt will come to the king of Greece to sign a treaty. However, the king of Greece will betray her and capture her. Her father, the king of Egypt will try to save her, but his armies will fail, and he will have to surrender to the king of Greece."

"Years later, a son of the King of Egypt will arise to the throne and will gather a large army to attack the kingdom of Greeks to take revenge. He will attack the fortresses of Greece, succeeding in defeating them and conquering them. Their princes, their coveted vessel of silver and gold, he will bring to captivity in Egypt, and he will remain in power for years longer than the king of Greece."

"The new generation of sons of the king of the Greece will gather armies and attack the king of Egypt. They will wage war between them and the king of Egypt will gain lands and treasures. The fight will be bitter, and the victory will not go to the king of Greece at that time."

"The king of Greece will return to his land with a vengeance in his mind, and raise a much larger army than the first time and will attack Egypt again. Your people will join the battle, helping Egyptians, against the invaders from Greece, but they will be defeated. The king of Greece will come to the land of Israel and will destroy it with his army."

"The king of Greece, Antiochus, will give an order to the general of his army to kill the nation of Israel. He will issue a decree against Israel, and he will command his General, Phillip, to kill whoever identified himself as a Jew, but he will not succeed, because Prince of Israel, Mattathias, son of Johanan, will rise and defeat the Greeks. He will succeed to break the Greek yoke in Israel."

A little army of Israel, here, will defeat the mighty Greek army.

"After cursing God and people of Israel, the king Antiochus will die a horrible death. While on route to besiege Jerusalem, he will contract an illness that will give him evil boils all over his body, and his limbs will start to fall off. He will order to be turned back to his city of Antioch, but will die on the way there."

Although God knows when and how the evil person

will come to earth, because He allows it to come in order to punish us, when the evil is done with his evil deeds, they always meet a horrible death.

"One who removed the Greek oppressor from the land of Israel, prince Mattathias, will strengthen himself in his base of the mount of Modin, for he will be the prince and a mighty man, as well as his descendants in distant future, the Hasmonians. However, his kingdom will not last over the dispute and jealousy with other Jewish princes, Hyrcanus and Aristobulus."

"Then the kingdom of Rome will come to power during King Titus' reign. The mighty Greek kingdom that was inundating and powerful before will be defeated."

"King of Israel will form a treaty with the Romans, but will be ultimately betrayed by them. They will take over the kingdom of Judah by turning the Jewish prince against his own brother. That is how evil works; through sweet talk, promises and lies to take advantage of human weakness. Jewish prince Hyrcanus will form an alliance to help the Romans against his brother Aristobulus, who will rule in

Jerusalem. However, Israel will not be subject to destruction in those days. That will happen later, in the days of King Agrippa, son of Agrippa of the seed of Herod."

"After the war, King Titus will return to his land with many possessions. At that time, some troops in the Roman army will rebel against Titus and weaken him. Once this evil king returns to Rome, he will brag about making the Jews abandon the covenant with God and spilling lots of innocent Jewish blood."

"Later, the evil King Titus will send his officers to Jerusalem, and the king of Israel, Agrippa, will be slain. They will destroy the city of Jerusalem, and they will profane the holiest room of the Temple. They will abolish a daily ritual sacrifice to God, and among abominations and disgusting things, they will place a dumb statue in the holy of the holies."

It teaches you here that to serve a statues or icons is very dumb.

"The evil Jews, who will join Titus and betray their fellow Jews, he will flatter with lies and promises of riches, to convert them to his pagan religion. Together they will write a new book [Here is the Introduction of the New Testament.], to serve their pagan god, claiming that there is a new covenant with the real God."

"However, the devout people of Israel will not believe the deceit and the new book. They will adhere to the covenant with the real God and the Book of Creation and will not abandon it, regardless to the offers of bribes and threats of Titus and his armies. The wise people among the good Jews will understand what happened, and try hard to teach the truth to the common people and encourage them to adhere to it, and not to listen to Titus' lies. They will try to convince them not to convert to the pagan religion, and not to serve the pagan "god". Some of these good Jews will suffer and die from the sword of the enemy, and some will be exiled to a faraway land. Some of them will manage to escape death by bribing the greedy enemy. Those righteous Jews are destined to receive their reward for their righteousness in the end of days. Good people go through hardship in their current lifetime, but their reward is eternal tranquility in the end."

"In distant future, many people will read this revelation of the end of days, and will try to calculate the time of the end, to know when the redemption is coming, but will fail. However, when the end of this world draws near, the wise people will be able to calculate the time of the end, to inform people about it."

"The kingdom of Rome will do as it wishes for many years, and will magnify itself. It will succeed until the fury is spent and the wrath of God turns from Israel. The kingdom of Rome will not put its mind to God, God of Abraham, Isaac and Israel, his forefathers, and nation of Israel. Before Titus' arrival many people were converting to Judaism, because they realized that the Jews were blessed. Titus will kill and exile many righteous Jews. He will corrupt many people and spread his religion. He will apportion land and dominion to those princes who honor his pagan "god" and convert to his religion. To spread his religion all over the world, Titus will use threats as one option and bribes as a second option. To those greedy people and princes, who covert to his religion, he will give land and riches. Here is how the evil works; he'll come to you and tell you: you have a choice; you can join me and I'll make you rich, or oppose me and I will destroy you. The weak minded always choose the first option. He will order to construct many churches of worship to the pagan god, all over the world. "

"This will continue until the set time of a decree, when the punishment period of the Jews expires. When the time of redemption draws closer, the kingdom of Egypt will attack Rome. The kingdom of Rome will overpower the kingdom of Egypt and will invade the land of Israel again, and many people will die. Rome will rule over broad lands and magnificent treasures and erect its worship places between the great seas of the world, and the beautiful Gods mountain in Israel, where Moses received the Book of Creation. However, it is already destined that the kingdom of Rome will come to an end, and no future leader will help it. The Roman Empire will eventually crumble."

That is the reality that we live today. The kingdom of Rome; aka the Christian world, is divided by many countries, and it is crumbling.

"There will be a long time of waiting. The ruling of abomination of the pagans will endure until the God's decree of the end of the days comes true. In that period of waiting, the world will degenerate to a faithless, materialistic and cruel world. When the decree of the end of the world is fulfilled, time will arrive for the damnation, destruction and extermination of the pagans and idol worshippers, in the days of King Messiah."

We learn here that the idol worshippers and the pagans will meet a horrible death and extermination at the end of days.

"At that time, Archangel Michael the chief archangel, who stands over the children of Israel, will be silent like a mute person for a long time. He will be silent because he knows that he does not have to defend your people anymore. God has already issued the final judgment for the end of days many years earlier"

"When the prophecy comes true, the final war will begin between kingdoms of Gog and Israel. The nation of Israel will be attacked by the kingdom of Gog, Kingdom of Magog, and their allies. After a long and brutal war, there will be time of a great distress in the nation of Israel. Your people will reach a tipping point in the war; they will have nothing left to keep or to abandon. At that point, they will be badly outnumbered and will be losing the war. At the meantime, in heaven, there will be accusations against Book of Creation scholars, by the Archangels of the different nations, defending themselves in front of God. They will be begging and pleading for survival as they entreat Creator not to destroy their nations for the sake of Israel. "

"Their pleading will not prevail, because Creator has made the whole universe for the righteous people to inherit it. The righteous people are the faithful Jews and the people who follow the commandments. However, those other nations will be pagans, perverted people and wicked people. That is why Creator has already issued the Judgment against those nations many years earlier. Just in the last moment of defeat, your people will be saved. The kingdoms of Gog and Magog will be destroyed, and all the good people of Israel will escape, everyone who is inscribed in the Book of Living for their good deeds. The righteous Jews will receive the kingdom, and the prophecy will be fulfilled."

Every time that we go sleep, angels interface with our soul and upload all the information. Our good deeds for that day are weighed against the bad deeds. In the end we will be judged.

"And many, who are dead, will come alive. Some of them will be the good Jews. They will live an eternal life. Some wicked people, who committed serious transgressions, will also be brought back to life for eternal disgrace and disgust. They will live in hell for eternity."

"In the new world that will be established, the wise people will shine like brightness of the sky because they will be the new stars. Those who bring many people to the ways of Book of Creation and goodness will be like stars forever and ever. They will travel around the world and teach Book of Creation and God to the remaining population of the world."

"And you, Daniel, close up the words and seal the book until the time of the end. At that time, people who remain in the new world will receive extraordinary technological and spiritual knowledge. They will become ultimately wise and advanced."

[The technological and spiritual knowledge that we possess today, is not even a tip of an iceberg, compering to what we will receive in the end of days.]

Daniel looked around, and noticed that there were two more angels. One was standing on one side of the river, the second one on the other side. Archangel Gabriel, who was explaining the future events, turned to Archangel Michael, who was hovering over the water, and asked him, "How long will it be until the secret end?"

[It is obvious that angel Gabriel knew the secret End, but because his humility, he wanted angel Michael to be involved.]

Archangel Michael raised his arms to heavens, and he swore by the life of this world, that in time of two times and a half, and when the enemies have ended shattering the strength of the righteous Jews, and the Jews have nothing left to keep or to abandon all this will end. This decree was necessary by God, to merit the destruction of the bad nations and to punish the bad Jews in Israel.

Daniel heard the words, but did not understand their exact meaning and ask the angel, "My lord, what is the meaning of this?"

The angel said, "Go Daniel. The calculations are hidden until the redemption is near. Nobody will understand the timing of the redemption until then. These calculations will be clarified and whitened, and many people who practice Book of Creation's commandments, will be purified by them, to understand them and know that the redemption is near. That knowledge will give them an extra incentive to observe the commandments. "

"The perverted people and the pagans will pervert the calculations and claim that the redemption is not coming. They will not understand and realize what would be going on until the last minute. However, the wise people will understand when the time of the end arrives."

[By the time the end of the world comes, most of the pagans and idol worshippers will be blinded by material things.]

"And from the time the daily sacrifice was removed and the silent disgrace of the mute statue was placed in the Temple, is one thousand, two hundred, and ninety. Fortunate is the person, who waits and reaches the days of one thousand, three hundred, and thirty five. Messiah will be revealed and then be hidden for 45 years and then be revealed again, when the time of the end arrives."

It teaches us here those 45 years before the end of the world, the Messiah will be born and known to righteous people. He will be 45 years old, when he will be anointed.

"You already passed the test of life, and you do not have to experience the hardship on this earth anymore. You will be awakening to life, when the redemption comes, and you will live with the righteous people like yourself, forever and ever..."

Daniel lost consciousness, and when he awoke, the angels were gone.

Daniel also prospered in the time of Kingdom of Cyrus the Persian, who was a son in law of Darius, and lived a long life. He spent years writing about his experiences as best as he could, for future generations.

Right now, Daniel's soul is resting together with all the righteous people, and he is waiting for the judgment of the End of the World to be fulfilled.

The book of truth

I wrote this book because the end of the world is drawing near. I want people to get inspired, and improve their situation. Studying the information in the original Bible, I came to the conclusion that at some point in the past, God already saw every possibility of the future. At that moment, He realized that the human depravity to faithlessness in the future was assured. He observed that, in all the possible futures, people got worse and worse, and wound up destroying each other. At that same time, God also realized that a small group of people would remain faithful until the end. Because of these special people, God did not give up on men. At that day in the history, Creator has issued the final judgment for the mankind. This is what this book is all about.

Although I have a strong original Hebrew roots, the Bible study is extremely difficult because it is extremely vague at times. The scripture is written in the most efficient and elegant style that only the wise people can understand. In order to remain faithful to the original story and to allow the public to understand it, I had to conduct a thorough research.

What is the Book of Creation?

This is a Book of Daniel Interpretation from the Book of Creation. Unlike the other stories, this one is committed to the original Book of Creation and tells it exactly the way it is, without doctoring! Secondly, it has the calculation of the secret End of the World timing in it.

The Book of Creation is the actual Manual that Creator gave to the Jews. It is the perfect book of wisdom. It has all the secrets of life encoded in it. It is inscribed in the most sophisticated and elegant manner, and designed in a way that only the wisest of the learned can fully understand it. Even the Christians will agree that most of the interpretation they use come from the Jewish scholars, such as Maimonides.

There is only ONE Book of Creation in the world. It is primarily written in ancient Hebrew! A small part of it is written in Aramaic, a language which is no longer in use. That means that all the Hebrew copies are identical! Jews would not dare to change one dot in it because they consider it an abomination.

An average Joe reads the Book of Creation literally, but

that is wrong. Every sentence that sounds simple has a whole story behind it. After arrival of Christianity, thousands of years later, the Book of Creation got translated into many languages. Even with the best of intentions, translating the Book of Creation correctly is almost impossible. In addition, all the Christian versions are translations of translations, heavily edited, misinterpreted and distorted.

Just to give you one example of the most serious distortion, the original Bible does not offer a hint of Jesus as if he never existed! That is a serious problem, because the Book of Creation has all the Predictions of the future in it until the End of the World. The original Manual preceded Jesus by thousands of years. Then, who added him in? My answer is The Christians, of course. To explain differently, if someone translates this most sophisticated book in existence, the translation should agree with the original. Jews had Book of Creation thousands of years before Christians, and they certainly know what is in it!

There are thousands more of the mistranslation and edits in the Christian versions. Most of these mistranslations and edits are so distorted that they don't even come close to the original. They were written in over-simplified way, to teach their Christian doctrine. Another thing is clear - the New Testament and Christianity emerged approximately

300 years after a supposed death of Jesus!

Now let's add the fact that the Jews, who received the original Book of Creation from Creator, do not accept Jesus. Why? Because they know that Creator is Omnipresent. That means that Creator lives in the past, present and future simultaneously. They know that Creator is perfect in a way that human mind could never understand. That means that Creator never makes mistakes, and He never changes His mind. They believe that Messiah will appear once. Therefore, the Jews observe all of the 613 commandments with conviction, to create a good and moral society, free of crime, hate and evil. This way, they can find a favor in the eyes of Creator, to be saved in the end of days.

To explain it differently, the Jews believe that Jesus got introduced by the idol worshipers and the pagans. In the eyes of Creator, the idol worship is as immoral a transgression as a murder. He warns against it almost in every page of the Bible. Add to that Christian churches' bloody history in the last 1700 years, which killed hundreds of millions of people. Add to that the crime, the violence, depression, and immorality that we have today. After one connects all the dots, they can make decisions about their life and future. Book of Daniel prophecy explains the current situation in the world, and the

Christianity. The information is right there. It sticks out like an elephant; and it is very hard to miss it, unless one distorts the story beyond recognition. I stayed true to the only true Bible, which is the Book of Creation.

The fate of the world nations

This book demonstrates that God is true. It also shows what it means to be faithful. It means that you will risk your life, in order not to break God's commandments. You should not break the commandments for the sake of your employer, spouse, money, fear of death, etc. That is how you get the attention of God.

Book of Creation indicates that the whole universe was created for the righteous people. The righteous people are the ones that truly have faith, and follow the commandments with the conviction.

It is clear that pagan practice and idol worship is the root of evil. It is strictly prohibited by God. Through the 5000 years of the Bible history, God's wrath is aroused, because people serve statues, icons, and idols. The Bible calls it silent abomination, and dumb. Do some of you think that God suddenly changed His mind about it, and became a pagan God? It is one thing believing in Jesus, but making his idols and others, and serving them, is idol worship. Jews have hundreds of saints and righteous people who spoke to God, but they do not worship them, do not pray to them, nor serve them. Those people were just humans! The same thing goes for the king Messiah. The Bible indicates that Christian religion was founded by Titus, who was the Satan in the flash.

Jews believe that Jesus has no connection to the real God. Jesus is the pagan "god". Jesus concept was created by mistranslating ad distorting the passage in the Book of Isaiah in the Book of Creation. Real God is Omnipresent and Infinite. He never breaks His rules, He never makes mistakes, and He never breaks His rules! He can't have children, because He is the universe itself. He is absolutely righteous beyond the understandings of the puny men. By doing away with Gods commandments, Christians introduced evil to the world. On the other hand, the Muslims have their own pagan "god", Muhammad.

Messiah did not come yet. It will happen at the end of this world. God makes his decisions after checking an outcome of every possible future. Everything was already pre-destined 2500 years ago. When Messiah comes, he will give the kingdom to the Jews and people who practice the commandments. These chosen people will become God's partners in control of this universe.

Out of the people that do not follow the commandments, some will face destruction, and some will live in the eternal disgust and abhorrence, which is hell. That means that the real hell was not established yet.

The souls who already achieved God's desired state of higher existence, like Daniel and other righteous people, are kept in a dream state until they come back to life at the redemption time. In God's kingdom the chosen ones will live forever, and the ones that died will come back to life.

After the End of the World, there will be only one ruling government in the world. All the countries that exist today will be gone.

The world will belong to the righteous people. The evil inclination of the people will be eliminated.

We find out that God knows your thoughts. You can fool people, but you cannot fool Him by pretending that you are doing the right thing. You need to mean it. We also find out that God decides which king or president will rule.

The Bible says that the kingdom that will exist at the time of redemption is the extension of the kingdom of Rome (also named Edom and Gog), the Christian world, which is divided by USA and European Union, divided by many countries, and other countries (kingdoms) of Assyria (Arab world), Persia (Iran), Greece, Egypt were given extension of life until the set time. The kingdom of Gog is what will remain of the Christian world, and some of the Muslim world under the leadership of Iran. In the final war, they will attack Israel.

In that period of waiting, anyone has a chance to join the Jews and start practicing the commandments, to secure their place in the kingdom of God. Think about it, if you let the commandments go, and do not practice its principles, your next generation and the following ones, will only degenerate to a worse and worse state of being, of dishonesty, immodesty, crime, etc. The 2nd commandment states about pagan worshipers, "visiting the iniquity of the fathers upon the children unto the third and fourth generation of them that hate me." Jews follow 613 Commandments. All the other people need to follow, in order to be saved, is the 7 Noah ide laws!

The Bible also says that Jerusalem will always exist until the set time of redemption, when it will become the KINGDOM OF God.

God's final goal is to establish a place on earth like the Garden of Eden, where only good people, who are FREE of Crime, Hate, Envy, Evil, will exist.

Most pagans and atheists will be eliminated from existence. The ones that have earned an extra punishment by committing serious transgressions will live in a reality of eternal suffering and hell, without a chance of any hope, ever.

I hope that I was able to inspire you by telling you about standards that God is expecting of mankind. Look around you and observe the state of the world.

Despite all the advances in science and sociology, the world is becoming worse because people disregard the commandments.

Instead of glorifying and appreciating the elderly, the wise, the faithful, this society glorifies people that are shameless materialistic whores. All this was foretold in the Bible.

Look around you. If I am wrong, would tiny Israel still exist with its might? Jews are only 0.02% of the world population but have many stars, leaders of the world, famous scientists, economists, sociologists, entertainers, lawyers. Is it a coincidence that stars like Albert Einstein, Sigmund Freud, Nostradamus, Baruch Spinoza, Marvel, Gustav Hertz, Melvin Calvin and thousands more come from this tiny nation? Is it a coincidence that the majority of innovations today come from Israel?

Is it a coincidence that the world is practicing Jewish religion in different variations?

Is it a coincidence that most of the laws of the land

are based on Book of Creation principles?

The evidence and information in Jewish Bible is undeniable even for an atheist or a hardcore Christian. This book was written almost 2500 years ago, and it is 100% true. I hope that you are inspired and will try to improve your ways and invest in your future. Think about the reward. All the suffering and hard work in this lifetime are well worth the reward in the end. At that time, you will become a full partner of God.

JewishPathways.com

Chabad.org

Aish.com

http://www.jewish-history.com/cresson/cresson04.html